CW00418401

IN THE
PALM OF HIS HAND

An inspiring collection of poetry

Kate is always happy to connect with readers. You can access Kate's social media platforms via her website:

www.katebrumby.co.uk
eBook available

f @PoetBrumby

🐦 @PoetBrumby

📷 @Kate_Brumby_Poet_Author

IN THE
PALM OF HIS HAND

An inspiring collection of poetry

KATE BRUMBY

First published in Great Britain in 2019 by:

DAISA & CO

Westfield Lakes, Far Ings Road, Barton upon Humber
North Lincolnshire, DN18 5RG, England

Written by Kate Brumby
Copyright © KATE BRUMBY 2019
Text copyright © KATE BRUMBY 2019. All rights reserved.
No part of this publication may be reproduced, stored in a retrieval system,
transmitted, or copied in any form or by any means, electronic, mechanical,
photocopying, recording or otherwise, without the prior written permission of the
publisher and copyright owner.

Pictures are reproduced by permission of the author unless otherwise stated. Every
effort has been made to trace copyright holders. The publishers would be pleased to
rectify any unintentional omission in subsequent printings.

The moral right of the Author has been asserted.

ISBN 978 1 9164928 6 8

A CIP catalogue record for this book is available from the British Library.

Book typeset by:
DAISA & CO
www.daisa-co.com

Printed in England

This book is made from paper certified by the Forestry Stewardship Council (FSC).
An organisation dedicated to promoting responsible management of forest resources.

I dedicate my poetry collection to Joan Brumby, my Mum and best friend.
If I had been blessed with a child, I would have liked to have been a Mum just like you.

Contents

Foreword

Abide With Me   1

Commission   2

Mindfulness   4

Back to the Cross   5

Definition   6

Love Alone   8

Moved   9

Disappointment   10

God's Guiding Hand   12

Receive My Blessings   14

My Soul   16

Healing Waters   17

Pure Love   18

Always the Same   20

Strength in Love   21

Rest in Me   22

His Hands   24

God's Fold   26

Arise & Walk   27

Be Kind to Yourself   28

He Who Liveth   30

Redirected   32

Eternal Souls   34

The Presence of God   36

Just Love   37

A New Day Dawns   38

Yours   40

Say Thank You   42

Moral Compass   43

Be Perfect   44

His Touch   47

Which Way?   48

Thankfulness   50

Acquiescent Fortitude   52

Masks   54

Journey of Life   56

My Provider   57

Unto You   58

God's Love   61

I Will Go Before You   62

Complete Picture   64

Let Go & Let God   66

Love in Action   68

May You Help Me   70

Be Comforted   71

Sometimes   72

It is Not Easy   74

Love Everlasting   75

Soul Searching   76

No Limit   78

Protector & Guide   79

The Critic   80

Healed from Within   82

Not an Option   84

Only a Thought Away   87

He Has Overcome   88

Soul Longing   89

My Happy Place   90

Looking Ahead   92

Ever With Me   95

Acknowledgements   96

Foreword

Many years ago Kate invited me to contribute a short Foreword to her first book of poems. I felt privileged to be asked and what I wrote then is set out below. Much more recently an email arrived from Kate, inviting me to write a Foreword to another volume of poems.

I refused! Or rather, I explained to Kate that I didn't want to alter a single word in the earlier piece. If I were to make any alterations it would be to underline some words and put others in capitals letters - because the passage of time and life's experiences have given her work even greater depth. Keep writing Kate. Keep warming our hearts!

~

I was delighted when Kate's letter arrived inviting me to write an introduction to her book. Many have found inspiration from her poetry. The thing that strikes me so forcibly about Kate's poems is their deep sincerity; they come from the heart.

It has been a great privilege to see Kate grow in her Christian faith. It has not been an easy path and her faith has been tested many times. But it has stood the test and God has called her, and gifted her, to share her faith and her experiences through the medium of poetry.

May all who read these lines find the same strength and peace as Kate has.

**Revd. John Young,
Canon Emeritus of York
Minster and Author**

Abide With Me

Your hands are ever before me,
Open wide my whole ready to receive,
I hear You call my name, Lord,
"Come My child, come rest here with Me.

Remember I welcome you always,
No part of you do I turn away from,
Simply draw close to Me here,
And into my presence now come.

Rest with Me in the stillness,
Cast all cares and burdens aside,
Worry not about anything more,
Let us just together here abide."

Commission

As He draws close, I am gently unwrapped,
Each layer like an onion is removed,
He reveals all that is hidden and guarded,
And beneath He discovers my truths.

He judges not in size or in amount,
He only delights in what is seen,
And He draws Himself so very close,
As though there's nothing in between.

He tells me of His unconditional love,
Assuring me on Him I can now depend,
Feelings of inadequacy He tells to go,
Knowing I can do great things in His strength.

He reminds me of His presence,
That in each moment He goes ahead,
I can rely on Him being beside me,
And I need not feel anxious or afraid.

He commissions me to spread His Word,
Good News of salvation and eternal life,
To let Him release me of focus on self,
And willingly allow Him into my life.

Mindfulness

As I read Your Word dear Lord,
I am reminded I can do all with You,
And I in You will nothing lack,
As together each moment we come to.

I am urged to be content, my Lord,
Not to wish things, people, or life away,
But to rest and treasure each precious second,
Here and now and in the coming days.

Lord, may my mind be more positive,
That when faced with an obstacle ahead,
I would see it not as something hindering,
But as a wonderful opportunity instead.

Opportunity Lord to be Your witness,
Of who You are in my own life,
That others may see my heart and mind,
Filled with the peace and love of Christ.

Back to the Cross

"*Remember, any thought you may have,*
If it is not focussed on I your God,
Is a thought blemished – not of pure love,
And its path leads only back to the cross.

Remember, any word you may voice,
If I your God am not its focus,
Is a word blemished – not of pure love,
And its path leads only back to the cross.

Remember, any task you choose to undertake,
If it is not done for My name's sake,
Is an action blemished – not of pure love,
And its path leads only back to the cross.

For any thought, word, or task,
Which does not on Me first focus,
Is marred by a selfish world,
For whom on the cross I was killed."

Definition

How easy it is to define ourselves by the good
left undone,
How easy it is to define ourselves by the race not
completely run,
How easy it is to define ourselves by the way we
stand and stare,
And somehow appear not to see all the needs
that are ever there.

Surely, this is a time to redefine ourselves as
Christians set apart,
Ready and willing to serve one another
with true and contrite hearts,
Surely, this is a time to define our lives as our
Lord asks us to do,
That we might be His instruments He wishes to
work through.

It's more difficult to define ourselves by the good
we have done,
It's more difficult to define ourselves by the race
we've partly run,
It's more difficult to define ourselves by the
needs we try to meet,
But oh what joy and blessing in so doing,
we and God reap.

Love Alone

Only love can bring light from darkness;
Only love can guide me on my way;
Only love can begin to understand me;
Only love can comfort my pain.

Only love I ask you to offer;
Only love will see me through;
Only love – that is all I need;
And love is all I can give to you.

Moved

Moved, to draw near to You,
Moved, to be still and quiet,
Moved, to voice not a word,
Knowing to speak only with my heart.

Moved, not to lean on my own understanding,
Moved, to wait on You, O' Lord,
Moved, to listen to Your counsel,
Anticipating blessings outpoured.

Moved, to dwell in Your presence,
Moved, not to hurry away,
Moved, to rest and to shelter,
As to You, my God, I now pray.

Disappointment

Disappointment when a promise is broken,
Disappointment when false words are spoken.

Disappointment when I am let down,
Disappointment when I am left alone.

Disappointment when I am betrayed,
Disappointment from what people say.

Disappointment when I don't seem to cope,
Disappointment when I seem to lose hope.

Disappointment when I fail to see,
The greater disappointment is actually me.

Me, the one who expects so much,
Me, the one too quick to judge.

Me, the one who fails perspective to keep,
Me, the one who does assumptions make.

Lord, I pray you'd help me to focus on You,
And be prepared to hear Your truth.

That disappointment is not how You feel,
As here at Your bidding I now kneel.

You only wish for me to learn, be wise,
And look at self and others with Your eyes.

To know all in Your sight are valued equally,
And we are always loved unconditionally.

God's Guiding Hand

My life is in Your hands, Lord,
You alone can forgive my sin,
You alone can take my brokenness,
And with Your love heal deep within.

Lord, I have felt so heavy laden,
Trying to carry all my cares and woes,
I have thought I could manage,
But every day troubles seem to grow.

Lord, I have felt so undirected,
Not knowing which way to turn,
But I must await your timing,
And patience like Yours now learn.

Realising enough is enough, Lord,
I must give all over to You,
And ask that You would take my hand,
And the next phase guide me through.

I set my eyes on You, Lord,
No longer running from pillar to post,
You are now my firm foundation,
In You I completely put my trust.

Receive My Blessings

"My healing is not to be struggled for,
Nor is it something for which to strive,
My healing is just to be trusted,
In each and every part of your life.

There is no need for you to worry,
Know, no job is too difficult for Me,
Just open your hands, My dear child,
And My blessings now graciously receive.

Receive My blessing of reassurance,
That you are precious in My sight,
And that I am always with you,
Never will I leave your side.

Receive My blessing of strength,
To sustain you in all you do,
Making you strong in weakness,
Allowing My will to be fulfilled.

Receive My blessing of peace,
To calm and still your soul,
Remember I, your Lord and God,
Your every need fully know.

Receive My blessing of joy,
Let it well-up within your heart,
May your happiness be infectious,
As your smile to another you impart.

Receive My blessing of love,
May it freely flow through you,
That you and all whom you meet,
May gentleness and power know.

May My blessings bring healing,
In each and every part of your life,
As you continue to trust in Me,
And cease to struggle and strive."

ell

My Soul

Lord, may You and I pray for my soul,
Lord, that by You it would be made whole.
Lord, that it would not be bruised
by careless thoughts,
Lord, that it would not be bruised
by spoken hurts,
Lord, that it would not be bruised by false words,
Lord, that it would not be bruised
by gossip shared.
Lord, may You and I pray for my soul,
Lord, that by You it would be made whole.
Lord, that it would not be bruised by situations,
Lord, that it would not be bruised
by gratifications,
Lord, that it would not be bruised by emotion,
Lord, that it would not be bruised by any person.
Lord, that You would reach down from above,
Lord, that You would heal with Your love.

Healing Waters

God's love is like a vast water,
Flowing out to me and to you,
And as God reaches out to all,
Each barrier He breaks through.

He wishes to draw ever closer,
To heal brokenness and pain,
To bind all as sisters and brothers,
Reconciliation being His aim.

We are reminded that each is precious,
Worth much more than silver or gold,
And that God undoubtedly delights,
When love between us He beholds.

Pure Love

Pure love is never self-seeking,
Pure love focuses on other's needs,
Pure love is about sacrificing,
Pure love is God's gift to me.

Pure love is not tainted,
Pure love is condition free,
Pure love is kind and gentle,
Pure love is God's gift to me.

Pure love delights not in evil,
Pure love rejoices in truth,
Pure love is ever hopeful,
Pure love is God's gift to you.

Pure love keeps no records,
Pure love always trusts,
Pure love steadily perseveres,
Pure love is God's gift to us.

Pure love is not proud,
Pure love does not boast,
Pure love never fails,
Pure love God's gift I treasure most.

Always the Same

Yesterday, today, tomorrow the same,
The love of God for each remains,
Unchanging, relentless in His commitment,
God's love is beyond thought, limitless.

No matter what we do or what we say,
God is there beside us now and always,
Whilst others their affection away take,
Nothing can God's love for us ever break.

For God is all powerful and Lord over all,
In whatever situation He is mighty conqueror,
Neither death nor life separates us from Him,
Neither angels nor demons – no, not anything.

Nothing can separate us from God's love,
Nothing in the depths or in the heights above,
God is constant, loyal and always true,
His grace He freely lavishes on me and you.

Strength in Love

To find strength in love,
Is to reach out to another in need,
To find strength in love,
Is with Christ's eyes to really see,
To find strength in love,
Is to know what life truly means,
To find strength in love,
Is God in each breath that I breathe,
Lord, may I find strength in love,
As I say, "Here I am to be used,"
Lord, may I find strength in love,
My life bringing honour and praise to You.

Rest in Me

Silently He came to me in the night,
Soft and gentle His voice was then heard,
"It is I your Lord and Saviour,
My child, do not be afraid.

I come to reassure you of My love,
Of my presence each day of your life,
Of the joy you give Me always,
As you seek with Me to abide.

Strive not, and do not worry,
No matter how you feel you stray,
I am truly forever with you,
I will never from you turn away.

It saddens Me to see you suffer,
I do not wish for you to grieve,
For once you have repented of sin,
It is gone and from it you are freed.

I am able to take your burden,
As I did that day on the cross,
I am able to take guilt and shame,
The price paid, there's no more cost.

So, My child lay, sleep on now,
For the night is almost at an end,
Rest here now in My presence,
Know on My grace you can depend."

His Hands

On the same night as He was betrayed,
He took bread and gave thanks,
He also blessed the wine,
Taking each in His hands.

Those same hands bore pain,
The pain of His crucifixion,
As He took my place on the cross,
The cost for my salvation.

As I picture my Lord now,
And call to mind His deep scars,
I realise each is due to my sin,
The price of a soul marred.

Yet, He continues to accept me,
Though I daily betray and fail,
Yet, He continues to forgive me,
Though each sin strikes another nail.

I gaze upon my crucified Lord,
And I am in awe as I watch,
His hands stretched out before me,
He says, *"I love You this much."*

God's Fold

"Behold I am the gate of the sheep,
None may enter except by Me,
I call to each of you by name,
Offering Myself to you now fully.

I am for you, each and every one,
I have many blessings to bestow,
Come, that I may give to you,
Come to Me, come, draw close.

Rest here at the feet of Your Shepherd,
I am He that lay His life down freely,
That you may enter the presence of God,
And know His love for you completely.

God asks nothing, but you be yourself,
His love for you is unconditional,
Come, take the bread and the wine,
And may your life be whole and full."

Arise & Walk

Standing, curved, spine so very bent,
Then no longer stooped, my back made straight,
All cares and burdens now caused to relent,
And only on my dear Lord I now wait.

Wait to listen moment by moment passing,
Not wishing or needing to rush on ahead,
Each breath I breathe to me a blessing,
No more my heart feeling heavily weighed.

He touches me, I turn and then look,
I am His and He is my own dear Lord,
No longer alone, no longer misunderstood,
Together in partnership we walk forward.

Be Kind to Yourself

"Start the day by being kind to yourself,
Go steadily, take now your time,
Remember you are My Dear Child,
I chose you, you are Mine.

I will be alongside you today,
And the tomorrows yet to come,
I am not wishing to change you,
Only guide and gently you hone.

You'll be the best you can be,
As we will walk side by side,
Remember my cord is strong,
Together we are firmly tied.

My creative hands work in you,
And through you – look here see,
All that you and I have made,
Is of love and immense beauty.

I will open the hearts of others,
They will see what we have done,
And they too will be inspired,
And want to Me to closely come.

But remember be kind to yourself,
Do not worry or stress at all,
I'm your Lord and gracious Father,
Just come and settle as I call.

Lean not on your own understanding,
In faith receive of Me as I do you,
And be assured that together,
There is nothing too hard to do."

He Who Liveth

"I am He that liveth,
Come, My child, come,
That together we may go forward,
And one day I'll lead you home.

Each day we will reach out,
Reach out with compassion and love,
That no glory be with us,
But only with our Father above.

I live and give Life to others,
No more should man now weep,
Even over death I have conquered,
So that souls My father may reap.

In our Father's garden we sow Truth,
We work in uncomplicated simplicity,
We work that others might know Him,
And would all His gifts now receive.

So, My child, come to Me,
Take My hand in your own,
Know we have many tasks to do,
Before the day you'll be led Home."

Redirected

It's so easy to get lost without silence,
Forget to be still and listen to Your voice,
So many things distract and busy me,
Resting is often a neglected choice.
Yet, if I were to cease rushing,
And be more mindful in each day,
I know that I'd be more effective,
And also efficient in all my ways.
I am reminded that when kept busy,
I'm tempted to act in my own strength,
When things could be eased greatly,
If I would just on Your wisdom depend.
I know that I have a tendency,
To battle on like a tenacious soldier,
Ignoring that Jesus Himself offers,
My yoke to carry, my burdens to bear.
Lord, I know I grow ever weary,
Feeling fatigue and I am often confused,

As to why I'm so headstrong,
And reluctant to turn Lord, to You.
So, I ask that You'd help me pause now,
To give time to be quiet and be calm,
Willing to receive Your guidance,
And Your worry-soothing balm.
Lord, that I'd raise my hands towards You,
And also to You open up my heart,
From this moment my life changing,
As I seek You humbly and contrite.
Lord, I can do little in my own strength,
It's You I need to me now empower,
Not that I'd be raised up, Lord,
It is You who I want to lift up higher.
Higher in my priorities, Lord,
Above all else put foremost,
So that You are the light to my path,
And I no longer feel forlorn and lost.

Eternal Souls

Eternal souls are in the making,
God's hand is upon their lives,
Gently preparing their hearts now,
To receive His love and light.

The light which heals brokenness,
And brings joy where sadness once was,
As our Lord beckons each one,
And to each He draws close.

He places His hand out in blessing,
Saying, *"My child I died for you,*
And with the blood of My body,
I wash and make you new.

Know I am always with you,
And have been from the beginning of time,
Know you have always been special,
For you were chosen to be mine.

The road you walk may be winding,
There'll be much to absorb and learn,
But blessings will be abundant,
And your eternal life will be certain."

The Presence of God

Realise the presence of God,
Self-centredness now renounce,
Approach in sincere humility,
And Him as your Lord pronounce.

Realise the presence of God,
Request the Holy Spirit's aid,
That you might know God's will,
And on His desire hereby meditate.

Realise the presence of God,
Cast all your cares to one side,
Know He will deal with them,
As here in the stillness you abide.

Realise the presence of God,
Give to Him your thanks and praise,
For He has joined in union with you,
And your freedom He has proclaimed.

Just Love

Lord, what do I do
when those around ignore You?
Lord, what do I do when those around scorn?
Lord, what do I do when those around hurt?
Lord, what do I do when those around mourn?

Lord, I hear Your answer… *"Just love."*

Lord, what do I do
when my life seems heavy laden?
Lord, what do I do when others seem not to care?
Lord, what do I do when others rebuke You?
Lord, what do I do when others doubt prayer?

Lord, I hear Your answer… *"Just love."*

Lord, what do I do when I am rejected?
Lord, what do I do when I am misunderstood?
Lord, I hear Your answer so very clearly,
"My child, in all things… Just love."

A New Day Dawns

He held you as you slept and in waking
He is there too,
He will be by your side in
everything that you now do.

He goes before you preparing each step
that's ahead,
So your heart need not be troubled
but be calm instead.

He wants only the best for you,
see His word says so,
He gives you challenges only so you'll
develop and grow.

He also gives all that you require –
together you will succeed,
So your heart is warmed with each breath
you breathe.

Blessings lay ahead today, watch, listen and
you'll them find,
And later you'll share joy of a wonderful
spiritual kind.

Your facial smile will be deeper than that which
others see,
As your heart will over-flow as His love runs free.

Yours

Listening ears, open hearts and empty hands,
These we bring, Lord to You,
And offering ourselves to do Your service,
Ask that You'd commission us to do Your will.

Lord, that we'd be able to really listen,
That our hearts would be ready to receive,
Lord, that taking nothing of our own,
We'd be available to others in need.

Lord, as we go with Your blessing,
We're called to remember Your great gift,
The gift of Your Holy Spirit's presence,
Enabling us to love without limit.

As we give ourselves over to You, Lord,
We're assured of Your power within,
And of the endurance of Your infinite love,
Flowing through as an endless stream.

Lord, we go to do Your bidding,
To be channels of Your grace and love,
Not that we'd be praised dear Lord,
But You our Father above.

Say Thank You

At close of day do you reflect,
And ponder upon the hours gone?
Do you thank God for blessings,
Or simply nightwear adorn?

I wonder if as dawn breaks,
And a new day begins,
If you then of God's gifts,
Graciously give thanks to Him?

Just imagine if each morning,
God decided to keep things back,
All gone unacknowledged,
What would you think of that?

Thank goodness God doesn't do this,
He does not punish in that way,
But you might want to consider Him,
In case He chooses to one day.

Moral Compass

It is not easy deciding which way to go,
Even the right thing to do is not known,
Sometimes it's easier to go with the tide,
Than swim against it and be all alone.

I need to be aware of my moral compass,
That which sets me on the right track,
That keeps me buoyant during adversity,
And from endeavour not cease nor slack.

I need to be mindful and listen,
To the voice which guides from within,
So as to not be tempted to seek false light,
Or be drawn in and down by dark sin.

Be Perfect

"Be perfect as your Father in Heaven is perfect,"
Crumbs, to do this seems an awesome task,
How can I compare myself to You, Lord?
As I kneel and know so much I lack.

But You seem to look past my wretchedness,
And gaze upon me with pure simplicity,
And with Your deep love and care, Lord,
You graciously ignore my human frailty.

I realise to be perfect is not a command,
It's an invitation to draw close,
Closer to You my Lord, and Father,
As Your direction and guidance You show.

Your hand laid gently upon my life,
I realise You wish only the best for me,
Working within to refine I Your child,
Into all You would wish me to be.

You still wish me to be myself,
I am fearfully and wonderfully made,
And knowing me even in the womb,
Each path ahead of me You've paved.

Paved as You have gone before me,
Bonded with Your care and Your blood,
That I might realise Your purpose,
As I take each step now onward.

Sometimes it's easy to feel despondent,
As I'm faced with the tests of life,
Sometimes I've felt I'm in a tunnel,
With little sign of a light.

But Lord, I have experienced Your power,
And know that even when I can do no more,
All I need do is be still and quiet,
And in faith Your name gently call.

You've never failed me, dear Lord,
You've always done what You've promised,
And I know when You say *"Come,"*
I will richly and deeply be blessed.

His Touch

A touch that heals the broken heart of man,
A touch that takes away all burdens.

A touch speaking when words fail to,
A touch which pierces through to inner souls.

A touch full of love and compassion,
A touch sincere and of truth.

A touch able to conquer even death itself,
A touch of strength and so powerful.

A touch of life-giving radiance,
A touch of gentle simplicity.

A touch offered with no condition attached,
A touch that we might all receive.

Which Way?

We celebrate the birth of Christ Jesus,
At Christmas time with great cheer,
We rejoice in His resurrection too,
But what about the rest of the year?

Do we just go to church on Sundays?
Perhaps weddings and funerals now and again?
Are we influenced by bad weather?
Is our absence marked by rain?

God wants much more of us than this,
He wants to meet with us each day,
To seek His will in all we do,
To be moved by His Spirit to pray.

God calls us to make a commitment,
We must love as He so loves us,
To be there for one another,
And seek the common good.

Today, let us seriously consider,
As we stand at the crossroads of life,
Who or what it is we are serving,
Do we acknowledge Jesus' sacrifice?

Are we walking the road of a Christian?
Is it as agnostic we will stay?
Do we wish to proclaim Atheism?
The decision is ours... Which way?

Thankfulness

There's always something to be grateful for,
An encouraging word, a reassuring touch,
It's the small gestures of kindness from others,
Each day that mean so very much.

I pause to mindfully reflect in this moment,
I look around, above, and below to what's near,
I ask to be awakened to Creation's beauty,
And to savour all sounds and the silences I hear.

May my day not be void of compassion,
Others too have wants that need to be met,
It's not that I'm less important or insignificant,
For outward evidence of value I need not fret.

There's always something to be grateful for,
I need to look at what is there, what I have,
And not dwell on myself and my anxieties,
No, better to reach out to another with love.

I will endeavour to provide words to encourage,
I will seek to reassure, and to also protect,
I'm sure as the day draws to an end be grateful,
And any insecurities and self-doubt I'll reject.

Acquiescent Fortitude

He did not seem to ever worry,
Nor wonder about his past,
Nor had it once occurred to him,
That the calm felt would not last.

She gave no concern of yesterday,
Nor wept over races not won,
Nor carried around grudges,
Or dwelled on things not done.

He feared not for his own future,
Nor that of family and friends,
Nor did his heart trip or falter,
Or believe life could one day end.

She never doubted her securities,
Nor imagined she'd be alone,
Nor had she ever considered,
That she'd be without a home.

They enjoyed living in the here and now,
Savouring each moment in time,
To do any other they subconsciously,
Likened to commitment of a crime.

They happily dwelt in the present,
As only children really can,
No thought of what is to come,
No focus on what has gone.

We can learn much from them,
As we ponder their and our world,
And now resolve when called upon,
To stand up, be counted and be bold.

We are reminded to be stewards,
Never to our responsibilities neglect,
To always shield the young and innocent,
And the defenceless seek to protect.

Masks

Why do we try to deceive each other Lord?
Why do we use energy holding up masks?
Do You think we will ever realise, Lord,
That human things do not last?

Lord, it seems we're far too busy to notice,
You offering to take charge,
And with gentleness and Your love,
Provide each of us with courage.

Courage to face what is troubling us,
And allow others our concerns view,
So we'd be open to Your counsel,
And of those whom You wish to use.

Lord, oh the release we'd then feel,
As our energy could be used elsewhere,
Wider in Your service, Lord,
To provide support and greater care.

Lord, help us to learn honesty,
To be blessed with humility and truth,
That we'd not attempt to deceive others,
And realise we cannot hide from You.

Journey of Life

"Know I'm able to keep your path straight,
As you travel the journey of life,
No need to be discouraged,
I never leave you alone to strive.

I remain ever close to guide you,
Along rugged paths that you'll meet,
I am walking along with you,
Feeling each bump beneath your feet.

Together nothing will overcome us,
You'll be equipped to face each fight,
And even in the darkest of hours,
You'll be led by My true light."

My Provider

When I was naked You clothed me,

When I was cold You gave me food,

When I was weak You gave me Your strength,

When I was rejected You accepted me,

When I was angry You calmed me,

When I was upset You comforted me,

When I was lost You found me,

At all times, Lord, You loved me.

Unto You

Unto You I commit my spirit,
Giving all that has gone before.
Unto You I commit my spirit,
And of my future I pronounce You Lord.

Unto You I commit my spirit,
Each moment I will not be alone.
Unto You I commit my spirit,
As to You I willingly turn.

Unto You I commit my spirit,
Into Your hands I place my life.
Unto You I commit my spirit,
Into Your keeping I place my heart.

Unto You I commit my spirit,
My own self to You I release.
Unto You I commit my spirit,
Open hands to receive Your peace.

Unto You I commit my spirit,
In the knowledge You are all I need.
Unto You I commit my spirit,
As Your grace I now receive.

Unto You I commit my spirit,
As Your child I take Your hand.
Unto You I commit my spirit,
Ready to do as You have planned.

Unto You I commit my spirit,
And ask on my journey You be guide.
Unto You I commit my spirit,
And ask You comfort when I'm afraid.

Unto You I commit my spirit,
May my faith and trust hereby grow.
Unto You I commit my spirit,
That Your Spirit through me would flow.

Unto You I commit my spirit,
 To You, Lord I give my all.
Unto You I commit my spirit,
In this moment and evermore.

God's Love

I know when I am in His presence,
Stillness consumes within and without.
Not a voice or a sound can be heard,
And only His love around me abounds.

A love beyond any words,
A love beyond comprehension.
A love which binds heart and soul,
A love without an ending.

A love which sustains each and all,
A love which is steadfast and true.
A love which conquers even death,
A love to see my whole life through.

I Will Go Before You

"I will go before you,
In all things I go ahead,
So My child, do not worry,
And do not feel afraid.

Even in the black and darkness,
There will shine a bright light,
With love guiding your footsteps,
As you travel the journey of light.

I will go before you,
In all things I go ahead,
So My child, do not worry,
And do not feel afraid.

There's nothing you'll face alone,
I am there within and without,
Holding you to Myself,
Never leaving your side.

I will go before you,
In all things I go ahead,
So My child, do not worry,
And do not feel afraid."

Complete Picture

It's all about God's own timing,
Not just mine or just yours,
God has an overview of the world,
Taking into consideration all of us.

Don't forget what effects one,
Also affects others in some way,
So we lift others known or not,
As we kneel and to our Father pray.

We ask that His Will would be done,
In our lives and all those around,
And that as we live our lives through,
A completer picture would be found.

That no more we'd view only through eyes,
But that our inner selves would also see,
That it was not for one man Christ died,
But for all He gave his life willingly.

So it is with God day to day,
He wants not just the best for me or you,
He wishes for all of the world to receive,
And towards Him to closer now move.

What seems like ill-timing for us,
Is only one view of the situation,
Only if we come to see as God does,
Will the picture be brought to completion.

Let Go & Let God

Lord, You've been teaching us to let go,
To let go and then to let You,
To stop trying to do things alone,
And be channels for You to work through.

We've felt ourselves haul up the reins,
As like a rider approaching a jump,
Attempting to gain some kind of control,
Not allowing ourselves to onward romp.

But Lord, You've revealed Yourself in this,
Showing us that if we sit back and relax,
You are able to guide our course ahead,
As You take us and our reins in Your hands.

Not that You then take over fully, Lord,
It's that you gently teach whilst alongside,
As we learn from Your guidance, dear Lord,
We know we need not hold on so tight.

Our gifts will then be used constructively,
Energy not wasted worrying about holding on,
Ready to face the challenges ahead,
As with You Lord You bid us to walk on.

Love in Action

Eliza sang of the needs she had,
Food, shelter, comfort to rest,
I wonder what we would ask for,
For our own lives to be blessed?

It is so easy to be complacent,
To not realise how much we have,
To be reluctant to see others,
And to their needs now give.

Our eyes may need to open,
To truly see others around,
For us to look with compassion,
Not sky-ward or to the ground.

Our hearts may need to soften,
Remembering we could be as they,
And but for the grace of God,
The hard road is where we'd lay.

Today, is chance and opportunity,
To help someone else we will meet,
Whether neighbour in our community,
Or stranger in the town or city street.

Let's have thoughts of generosity,
A willingness to others love,
Not to do little to help them,
But today give enough and above.

~For Eliza Doolittle~

May You Help Me

When all around seem to hate,
Lord, may You help me share Your love.

When all around appear sad,
Lord, may You help me share Your joy.

When all around appear at war,
Lord, may You help me share Your peace.

When all around appear cruel,
Lord, may You help me share Your kindness.

When all around seem disloyal,
Lord, may You help me share Your faithfulness.

When all around seem harsh,
Lord, may You help me share Your gentleness.

When all around seem undisciplined,
Lord, may You help me show self-control.

Be Comforted

She pauses at God's throne on high,
Where she will serve now only Him,
And greeting her He whispers, *"My child,*
My child, come, rest here within.

Never again will you hunger,
Never again will you thirst,
Never again will you feel sorrow,
Never again will you hurt.

I, the Lamb will be your Shepherd,
I'll lead you to the water of Life,
I will comfort, and I will bless you,
And wipe every tear from your eyes."

Sometimes

You are there beside me each day,
You are there beside me always,
You are there beside me showing the way,
So close beside You may I stay.

Sometimes I look over my shoulder,
Dwelling on what has gone,
How easily I forget, Lord,
That with You I can move on.

Sometimes I feel so heavy laden,
Not knowing which way to turn,
How easily I forget, Lord,
That with You my feet are firm.

Sometimes I cannot see before me,
Onward to what lies ahead,
How easily I forget, Lord,
That by You I will be led.

You are there beside me each day,
You are there beside me always,
You are there beside me showing the way,
So close beside You may I stay.

It is Not Easy

Lord, it is not easy to forgive,
Lord, it is not easy to forget,
Lord, it is only You can help me,
As my heart weeps with regret.

Lord, it is not easy to know honesty,
Lord, it is not easy to discern truth,
Lord, it is only You who can help me,
As my heart sighs confused.

Lord, it is not easy to wait,
Lord, it is not easy to be patient,
Lord, it is only You who can help me,
As my heart feels indignant.

Lord, it is not easy to have faith,
Lord, it is not easy to trust,
Lord, it is only You can help me,
As my heart is emotionless.

Love Everlasting

I am loved with an everlasting love,
Taking my whole being in Your arms,
And as I rest in Your Word, dear Lord,
I receive Your peace and Your calm.

No longer I need to fear, Lord,
For You are with me by my side,
Here to share in my joys, dear Lord,
Here to wipe away tears that I cry.

As I go Lord from this quiet,
May I continue to feel Your presence,
May I live a life of Your love,
As I on You have pure reliance.

May I be all you want of me,
May I unafraid Your love impart,
May I know that You reign in me,
Renewing and refilling my heart.

Soul Searching

Lord, You called me to be quiet,
To wait, be still, and to pray,
And with my whole being, Lord,
Listen to what You wished to say.

As You drew closer in the silence,
Lord, I felt Your hand touch mine,
All fears and anxieties were soothed,
And my heart was blessed with calm.

No longer did I feel alone, Lord,
For you sat there by my side,
Changing the negatives to positive,
Wiping away tears that I cried.

Gradually Lord I felt healing,
Healing of guilt, shame and hurt,
Even feelings of bitter resentment,
By Your love were dispersed.

I realised that from trial and troubles,
No one is ever promised to be free,
But in all we're asked just one thing,
To always look outward to Thee.

No Limit

As I look today at God's written word,
And read the healing of the boy of an evil spirit,
In my mind Jesus' voice can be clearly heard,
"My child remember faith has no limits."

How often it seems I fail to trust,
How I seem to lack belief day to day,
And as I sit with my Bible now,
It is to God I sincerely pray.

I ask that He show me more fully,
The truth He would want me to know,
That I would be as a tree planted firm,
With strong roots and fruitful shoots grow.

I also ask for His reassurance,
That in Him all is possible in life,
And even faith as small as a mustard seed,
Can move a mountain as if it is light.

Protector & Guide

"I am your shield and shelter,
I am the guide of your feet,
I will take you through each day,
In every moment your prayers greet.

Lean on Me in the next hours,
Take My hand, My dear child,
I will be there beside you,
Your steps and words to guide.

Remember, all children are precious,
Each has a special place in My heart,
Know I always bring to completion,
Anything that I choose to start.

I am moulding you gently,
I am equipping you for a role,
One day soon I will reveal it,
But until then only it I know."

The Critic

It's tempting to be the critic,
To join others in negativity and lies,
To describe she who succeeds in life,
As one who fails and does not try.

So often the one who's pointed at,
Is not the one who's truly judged,
As it is the one who is pointing there,
Is the one with a chip or a grudge.

To point a finger at she who's strong,
In an attempt to ridicule and pull down,
Misplaces what prompts the act,
A jealous smile appears as a frown.

For he or she who points with one,
Forgets three other fingers face themselves,
And criticism and negativity directed,
Is theirs to have not someone else.

Yes, it's easier to be the critic,
To join others in their bitter way,
Than inwardly look at the truth beneath,
Admit fault and "I am wrong," say.

Healed from Within

To be healed isn't necessarily outward,
For much goes on within not seen,
For our Lord does not judge physically,
He longs just that hearts be clean.

That hearts would be made holy,
Filled with His love and His truth,
Hearts that reflect His beauty,
As to Him we closer move.

He has promised us new bodies,
Which will no longer hunger or thirst,
Bodies transformed by peace,
Never again to feel pain or hurt.

How wonderful when the day comes,
When we His face will behold,
But let us not wish time away,
To work on earth, we are called.

He is calling each of us daily,
As our human bodies will permit,
To be channels of His love,
As upon His road we now set.

Let us remember here together,
That all are precious in His sight,
And that He judges not in appearance,
For He sees not only with His eyes.

He knows the beauty which lies within,
And touches all with His healing balm,
And gives us eternal assurance,
Saying, *"Be still, you are mine."*

Not an Option

To do nothing is not an option,
We have been called to do so much,
Each by name is asked to go,
And reach out with God's touch.

He has commissioned us to multiply,
To spread the news of His Word,
To be brave and yet be mindful,
As we go into the wider world.

He asks that we start within ourselves,
We our own life rhythms to write,
And as we draw strength from God,
We look outward to widen our sights.

In our community that we dwell in,
He'll equip and will each of us guide,
He has promised to go before us,
And each step to be by our sides.

We are called to serve our neighbours,
And in this be brave and bold,
Knowing that God prepares their hearts,
So that in us it's He they'll behold.

As we share with one and then another,
God's truth and love will be outpoured,
And more and more of His people,
Will help transform and reclaim His world.

We are asked to dream big and imagine,
Not limit our minds to what we have seen,
But to trust in God and His understanding,
And in His great power believe.

We are to wait, watch and be joyful,
As we witness to and see Him at work,
Knowing that His people can truly,
Change and fill the whole earth.

To do nothing is not an option, oh no,
For we each must do our part,
As we take the first step of many,
Here, tonight in our own hearts.

Let us encourage one another.
When things are hard or tough,
Not to waver from our resolve,
To continue to reach out with God's love.

Only a Thought Away

Lord, as I sit here in Your presence,
Here quietly at the foot of Your cross,
I realise You are always with me,
Your company can never be lost.

No matter it seems which way I turn,
As I travel the journey of my life,
You will ever be there with me,
As my friend, protector and guide.

I may at times ignore You, Lord,
From Your ways I may often stray,
Yet even in the times of dryness,
You are only a thought away.

He Has Overcome

"I have overcome the world,
There is nothing that defeats Me,
As My resurrection has shown,
Even from finite death I am free.

As I dwell in your being,
I am able to strengthen and sustain,
Providing courage and endurance,
Deliverance being my aim.

You will not face the future alone,
I will be there along the path you take,
I'm your shield, I'm your shelter,
I'm your guide each step you make.

There will be times of temptation,
There'll be feelings of being overwhelmed,
But do please remember, My child,
I have overcome the world."

Soul Longing

We two to become one, Lord,
For this my heart and soul long,
As within my being, Lord,
I know with You I belong.

Lord, I'm aware I need to awaken,
Your glory and grace to really see,
That I might now welcome, Lord,
Your Spirit to dwell within me.

I hear You say You wish to bless,
To give all that my soul needs,
And in drawing closer to me,
From all my fears give me release.

As You touch my hand, Lord,
I am aware of your strength and might,
Savouring this moment fully,
My acceptance now ends the fight.

My Happy Place

My happiest place is inside my head,
When at close of day I think,
Of all the blessings I've received,
And the joy each one brings.

I savour smiles and sunshine,
I recall laughter and words shared,
I mentally hug each person,
Who has shown that they care.

Inside my head I store memories,
So I will be reminded of who I am,
Each lovely moment treasured,
Whilst I am able...whilst I can.

There may be a time in the future,
I won't be able to recall very much,
So I hope that in my head I'll know,
That by others I have been loved.

I pray that my happiest place,
Will be filled like a library with books,
Today, and in each tomorrow too,
So I can at each blessing look.

Wherever your happiest place is,
I hope you will also know this truth,
That whatever in it that's special,
Is special because of one thing... You.

Like me, you'll browse shelves,
And in your mind's eye picture a place,
As though a dust cover or jacket,
Guarding printed words on a page.

I pray like me, you will savour today,
And enjoy thinking of a happy place,
And at close of day in your heart,
Give thanks to God for His grace.

Looking Ahead

In life there are many tribulations,
We may all have troubles ahead,
Some causing anxiety and raised emotion,
Other trials filling us with dread.

There is no rhyme nor any reason,
As to why we feel as we do,
But perhaps we need to remember,
With God we can all get through.

That challenges we have make us stronger,
To become the people God wants us to be,
And we are not ever asked to be alone,
He provides the help of the Trinity.

Together with God nothing can overcome,
Whether in the physical or spiritual realms,
Not if we hand control over to God,
And allow Him to take the helm.

He will guide us through all life's storms,
He will ride the waves and ebb the tide,
He'll dampen the main brace securely,
Never once moving from our sides.

No matter how choppy or undulating,
The route before us will be eased,
As we cling to Jesus, our life provider,
Fears and worries will begin to cease.

As we grow in faith and reliance,
We will be rewarded and by God blessed,
And the flag of celebratory victory,
Will be hoisted on our main mast.

Others will see our Lord in action,
They will want to rely on Him too,
And the world that we live in,
Will be transformed and made new.

If all turn to Christ and His power,
A mighty army will rise up as one,
And in the battle of good and evil,
God's way will be the winning one.

No hunger will be in any continent,
Each will have enough water and food,
Poverty will disappear in a blink,
Compassion and mercy will shine through.

Nation will no longer fight nation,
All men and women will live in peace,
And the unconditional love of God,
Will banish all hate and unease.

All for one and one for all will be shouted,
All equal, none deserted or bereft,
And the Lord God Almighty will proclaim,
"Behold My children, with whom I'm blessed."

Ever With Me

I heard You whisper my name, Lord,

So gentle and calm was Your voice,

You invited me into Your presence, Lord,

For You wanted me to draw close.

I knelt there at Your feet, Lord,

My heart yearning for Your touch,

As You stooped down to me, Lord,

And in Your grace, You lifted me up.

Acknowledgements

In many ways it is difficult to know where to begin with my thanks as so many people have encouraged and supported the publication of this poetry collection.

Primarily I thank my parents Frederick Thomas Brumby, my Pops and Joan Brumby my Mum.

Pops has provided an icon which is being used alongside my other marketing material, namely the logo for badges and other merchandise which is being sold to aid fund raising for Oikos, a local charity involved in the provision of a Food Bank and an ecumenical shop.

In the Palm of His Hand is dedicated to my Mum which I think says all I need to in way of how much she means to me.

Both my parents have instilled in me, in very different ways, that I can achieve anything I set my mind to; despite the diagnosis of Dyslexia in my early years, and other challenges I have faced.

My greatest encourager is my husband Mike, who listens almost daily to new verse and endless chatter about all things book, writing and poetry related.

~

My sincere and longstanding thanks to Canon John Young who was the first person to receive personalised verses in the form of a song when he moved from his role of Chaplain at the University College of Ripon and York St. John where I was studying Occupational Therapy, to being a full-time Evangelist.

John welcomed me as warmly when I contacted him prior to publication as he had almost 30 years ago. The world is all the richer for having such a gentleman, in all respects of the word, in it. John is always encouraging and uplifting whether in person or via email.

~

I have been very blessed to have a team of wonderful Beta Readers and encouragers.

My heartfelt thanks to them all for taking the time to read, comment, make suggestions, invite me to write for events, inspire poetry, and at all times support me in bringing this collection together and to publication.

Malcolm Bailey, Gloria Elwick, Alice Farman, Beryl Field, Giannina Foster, Judy Humphrey, Rev. Nichola Jones, Janet Kendrew, Mary Knaggs, Jennifer MacLaren, Kate Marr, Fr. Owain Mitchell, Jennifer Parker, Revd. Peter Thomas, Sylvia Thomas, Hilda Thorrington.

~

A special thank you to Sue Williams for providing the photographs for both my book and website.

~

Additional thanks to Giannina and Hilda who provide much needed assistance at talks and events and to Judy, my prayer partner – all of your generosity of time is appreciated more than I can say.

I give thanks to Daisa & Co. From the first meeting I knew that they would enable my dream of having my poetry professionally published to be achieved.

My Publishers have not only made it possible, they have done it in the most upbeat and enthusiastic manner anyone could imagine.

~

And finally my thanks to you Readers, and to those who contact me on social media – especially Sally Allister, Sue Baker, Karen Cohen, Rose Davies, Jean Davis, Alethea Dickinson, Carolyn Doyley, Patricia East, Sue Frendt, Alice Gilbert, Avis Hargreaves, Jill Haw, Cicely Kerry, Rebecca Lipcsei, Bonnie Poole, Mandy Riley, Marion Smith, Jill Tonge, Mandy Unduka, and Sharon Walsh.

I hope my poetry collection is enjoyed by all.

Blessings,

Kate

Gaelic Blessing

"May the road rise to meet you,

May the wind be always at your back.

May the sun shine warm on your face,

The rains fall soft upon your fields.

And until we meet again,

May God hold you,

In the palm of His hand."

Kate is always happy to connect with readers.
You can access Kate's social media platforms via
her website:

www.katebrumby.co.uk
eBook available

f @PoetBrumby

🐦 @PoetBrumby

📷 @Kate_Brumby_Poet_Author